Pure Intimacy

How Your Marriage Can Benefit from Natural Family Planning

Jason Evert

Pure Intimacy
Jason Evert
© 2019 Totus Tuus Press

All rights reserved. Except for quotations, no part of this book may be reproduced or transmitted in any form or by any means, electronic or mechanical, including photocopying, recording, uploading to the Internet, or by any information storage and retrieval system, without written permission from the publisher.

Unless otherwise noted, Scripture quotations are taken from the Revised Standard Version: Catholic Edition (RSV:CE) of the Bible, © 1996 by the Division of Christian Education of the National Council of Churches of Christ in the United States of America.

Totus Tuus Press
PO Box 5065
Scottsdale, AZ 85261
TotusTuusPress.com

Cover by Devin Schadt
Interior by Russell Design

Printed in the United States of America
ISBN 978-1-944578-75-6

Many couples have never heard an adequate explanation of why the Church seems "hung up" on the issue of contraception. As a result, many assert that the Church has no business in the bedroom, and wonder what a bunch of celibate men could possibly know about enhancing marital bliss. If the Church allows the antiquated "rhythm method" to avoid pregnancy, the argument goes, why not the Pill?

These are legitimate questions, and so they deserve serious consideration—which is the purpose of this booklet. Although not all couples feel the need to regulate births, you may have legitimate reasons for delaying pregnancy. If so, I presume that if there was a method of spacing births that was allowed by the Church, was ninety-nine percent effective,[1] cost little or nothing, and had no side-effects, you'd be willing to consider it.

You may be wondering, "What's the catch? If this method is so perfect, wouldn't every couple already be using it?" Most have never considered Natural Family Planning (NFP) because they mistook it for the ineffective "rhythm method." Others, upon hearing that NFP couples abstain from sex on certain days of the month, don't care to hear any more details. What they never heard was the difference between NFP and contraception when it comes to a person's marriage, body, and soul.

What is NFP?

Natural Family Planning is a method avoiding or achieving pregnancy by observing the changes in a woman's body that indicate her fertility. Any couple can pinpoint the woman's time of ovulation, and space births by abstaining from sex during the fertile period.

NFP is often confused with the less effective "calendar" or "rhythm" methods of the early 1900's. These methods involved counting a number of days from a woman's first day of menstruation to determine the time that she was presumed to be fertile. Such methods of avoiding pregnancy had high failure rates because they did not account for the fact that many women have irregular cycles and every woman's cycle is unique. NFP, on the other hand, is far more reliable. According to the *British Medical Journal*, "the accumulating data confirm that natural family planning can be as effective as any method of family planning [contraception]."[2]

Unlike the calendar/ rhythm method, NFP involves precise monitoring of a woman's fertility. Modern science has discovered that indicators of a woman's fertility include her temperature, the position of her cervix, and the nature of her cervical mucus. (However, not all forms of NFP use each of these indicators.)

Because NFP provides a deep understanding of the woman's cycles, it can also be used to detect fertility problems. If a couple has difficulty conceiving, the information they gather by monitoring the woman's fertility cycles will alert them to reproductive abnormalities and assist the doctor in treating the couple for these problems. Even if there are no difficulties in achieving pregnancy, NFP charts can help alert the doctor to other health concerns.

Because the Church does not expect couples to have more children than they can handle, NFP provides a safe, moral, and effective way to plan a family.

What difference will NFP make in my marriage?

Studies have shown that, unlike couples using other forms of contraception, couples who practice NFP have a divorce rate under 3 percent.[3] Some argue that this correlation exists because couples who use Natural Family Planning are often deeply religious, and such couples are less likely to see divorce as a solution to marital problems. While there is some truth to this, there are many reasons why NFP strengthens marriages, regardless of the couple's degree of religious devotion.

First, NFP deepens intimacy between spouses. As one woman who switched from contraception to NFP said, "I now know the true meaning of the word *intimate*."[4] Because NFP removes the "barriers" of contraceptive sex, the couple is given an increased sense of closeness—both physically and psychologically.

All-Pro NFL quarterback Philip Rivers pointed out that self-control "doesn't end when you get married. Chastity is still part of your marriage." He and his wife practice NFP, and he noted that "it can be hard as ever sometimes. But it makes us stronger and love each other more. It allows you to love in many different ways. . . . That part of our relationship has strengthened us."[5] Because NFP involves planned times of abstention from the marital act, it helps couples to find other ways of expressing affection to one another. As a result, the intimacy between them deepens. Even the act of abstaining from intercourse can be a loving gesture, since having more children at that time may not be best for the family.

Second, the necessity of practicing self-control keeps spouses from taking each other for granted. Since the spouses are not constantly sexually "available" to the other, the relationship is given space to breathe. In the words of one husband, "It's wonderful because it almost creates the honeymoon over and over again."[6] Such anticipation of the marital act intensifies its joy. Contraception does not offer this benefit, but instead weakens restraint and promotes self-indulgence, which is the opposite of self-giving love. Another husband explained, "[NFP] has called me to cherish my wife rather than simply desire her."[7] The Church echoes these remarks, saying that NFP "favors attention for one's partner, helps both parties to drive out selfishness, the enemy of true love, and deepens their sense of responsibility."[8]

Third, NFP encourages communication and understanding between spouses. Unlike other forms of family planning, NFP requires the man and woman to share responsibility for this aspect of married life. In turn, this offers the couple opportunities to discuss their plans and hopes for the size of their family. Because NFP requires a mutual effort, the man gains new appreciation about how his wife's body functions. Instead of suppressing her fertility in order to conform to his desires, the husband who uses NFP conforms his sexual desires out of reverence for the way his bride has been created.

Finally, when a couple is practicing chastity within marriage and obeying the Church's teaching on sexuality, they avoid any guilt or anxiety associated with the opposite life-style. The union of their wills with the will of God allows them to deepen their spiritual lives and love each other more perfectly.

I'm not sure my spouse will go along with this . . .

Understandably, the idea of abstaining from sex at times may not sit well at first. One husband shared with me that when he and his wife were experiencing fertility problems, her doctor asked them to abstain for a month, in order that he might assess her condition with greater precision. "A month?" the husband exclaimed.

The nurse in attendance happened to be a 70-year-old nun. She looked at the husband, nodded, and assured him, "You'll be all right." At that moment, he understood that he could survive a month of abstinence.

Abstaining from sex for a time is a normal part of married life, due to travel, illness, childbirth, or even simple consideration of an exhausted spouse. Healthy marriages survive these times and grow stronger, and NFP couples know from experience that the times apart serve to draw them closer together. However, research shows that NFP couples do not have intercourse less often than other couples. They just time it differently.[9]

Despite what some spouses may fear, endorsements of NFP are resounding from husbands as well as wives. One man explained to me that NFP "keeps the passion alive!" Another described it as "the best kept secret." In many cases, husbands find that their wives are actually more responsive after switching to NFP. I once received a letter from a wife who said that while she and her first husband were using contraception, she felt like a "toy or a recreational vehicle." She has since been married in the Church and has used NFP for years. In her words, "a chaste marriage is the ultimate!"

Now, when was the last time you heard a woman say that using spermicide is "the ultimate" or that, after getting an injection of Depo-Provera, she finally knew the meaning of intimacy? The enthusiasm has never been there, because deep down, no woman wants to contracept. Sure, she may want to delay pregnancy, and may seem content with the method. But despite how delighted women appear in birth control commercials, most women would rather not wage a chemical war against their own fertility.

For evidence of this, consider the following: One of the best ways to assess a couple's satisfaction with any family planning method is to look at how many couples continue to use it over time. For example, spermicides have a 42 percent annual continuation rate; the condom, 53 percent; the shot, 56 percent; diaphragms, 57 percent; the Pill, 68 percent.[10] What about NFP? Research of 1876 couples using the Creighton Model of NFP showed that it has an annual continuation rate of 89 percent—which is higher than any form of reversible contraception.[11]

Why doesn't the Church allow married couples to use contraception?

The Church will never force any couple to use NFP. Rather, the Church gently and firmly invites us to virtue. In the words of Saint John Paul II, "The Church and the world today more than ever need married couples and families who generously let themselves be schooled by Christ."[12]

To understand the moral problem of contraception, it helps to have an understanding of its history. Many assume that birth control was invented in the 1960's, but the practice is nothing new. Various methods of artificial birth control have been used for more than four thousand years. In ancient times, people would swallow potions to cause temporary sterility. Others would use linens, wool, crocodile dung, or animal skins as barrier methods; or they would fumigate a woman's uterus to keep her from bearing life. Even at the time of Christ, contraception was practiced among the Romans. In the Middle Ages, oral contraceptives included arsenic, lead, mercury, and strychnine![13] In the early 1930's, women's magazines even recommended using Lysol or athlete's foot medicine as a spermicide![14] However, Christians always stood out from such cultures because they refused to use contraception.[15] It was part of the Christian faith.

All Christian denominations condemned the use of contraception until 1930, when the Anglican Church decided to allow it in some circumstances. Their move was followed up by a similar endorsement by The United States' Federal Council of Churches. At the time, even the secular media was shocked by the idea that Christian churches would endorse contraception. The *Washington Post* predicted that such a switch "would sound the death knell of marriage as a holy institution by establishing degrading practices which would encourage indiscriminate immorality. The suggestion that the use of legalized contraceptives would be 'careful and restrained' is preposterous." Two days later, the newspaper added that such "departures from Christian teachings are astounding."[16]

Many Protestants agreed, such as Lutherans and Southern Baptists who called contraception "a twentieth century renewal of pagan bankruptcy," that would "prove seriously detrimental to the morals of our nation."[17] One Methodist bishop added that the decision to moralize contraception "certainly does not represent the Methodist Church, and I doubt if it represents any other Protestant Church in what it has said on this subject."[18]

Unfortunately, these protestations were short-lived, and Protestantism as a whole caved in on the issue. But the Catholic Church stood fast to the teaching of historic Christianity.

Why doesn't the Church "go with the flow"?

The modern world has trouble accepting the Church's stance on contraception because it doesn't understand the purpose of sex as God designed it.

Frank Sheed noticed, "Modern man practically never thinks about sex." He dreams of it, craves it, pictures it, but never pauses to actually *think* about sex. Sheed continued, "Our typical modern man, when he gives his mind to it at all, thinks of sex as something we are lucky enough to have; and he sees all its problems rolled into the one problem of how to get the most pleasure out of it."[19]

As Christians, we should give more thought to the matter, and consider what God had in mind when He invented sex. In the beginning, God created man and woman in his image and likeness. God is Love, and through the male and female bodies, this deep reality is made visible. As Saint John Paul II said long before he became pope, "God who is Father, who is Creator, planted a reflection of his creative strength and power within man. . . . We should sing hymns of praise to God the Creator for this reflection of himself in us—and not only in our souls but also in our bodies."[20]

When Adam and Eve became one flesh without shame, and obeyed God's plan to be "fruitful and multiply," they became an earthly reflection of the life-giving love of God.

For this reason, the Church teaches that s*ex reflects the life-giving love of the Trinity.* The Father, Son, and Holy Spirit are a union of persons whose love gives life. The same is true of a husband and wife. This insight, taught by Saint John Paul II's "Theology of the body," is a beautiful way to look at married love. It explains that God's plan for us to love as he loves is stamped into our bodies. So there is really only one question to ask when it comes to sexual morality: Am I expressing God's love through my body? The marital act as God designed it allows a couple to become an image of divine love! Through their love, they unveil the love of God.

This theme—of marital love being a reflection of God—is not new. Throughout the Bible, God's love for the Church is compared to a man's love for his bride. For example, St. Paul tells husbands that they should love their wives as Christ loved the Church, giving himself up for her "that he might sanctify her... that he might present the church to himself in splendor, without a spot or wrinkle or any such thing, that she might be holy and without blemish . . . . 'For this reason a man shall leave his father and mother and be joined to his wife, and the two will become one flesh.' This is a great mystery, but I speak in reference to Christ and the Church" (Eph. 5:24-27). This should lead us to ask ourselves, "If the one-flesh union of a husband and wife is a reflection of the love between Christ and his Church, where does contraception fit into the picture? What is contraceptive about Christ's love?"

The love of Christ is free, total, faithful, and life-giving. Similarly, during the wedding ceremony, couples publicly declare that their love is freely given, total, faithful, and open to life. When the newlywed couple consummates their marriage, their wedding vows and promises are spoken through their bodies. From then on, each act of lovemaking becomes a renewal of these wedding vows. But how can a couple give themselves *totally* to each other if they reject each other's fertility? How can they be *open to life* if they're taking drugs or using devices to sterilize the marital act? At the very moment the couple should be renewing their vows, they contradict them.

Therefore, contraception does not speak the "language of love," a message of complete self-donation. Its very nature is rejection—something not conducive to an intimate marriage. Every time she uses contraceptives, the woman is saying, "I want to make love to you, but I'm going to kill any sperm that come my way."[21] Every time a man uses a condom, he is saying, "I am protecting myself from you," or "I give everything to you, except for my fatherhood." Since the body reveals the person, a rejection of the body is a rejection of the spouse.

Some couples may struggle to understand this, because our culture has driven a wedge between the two purposes of sex: procreation and union (babies and bonding).[22] However, what God has joined, no one should separate. The couple who sterilizes an act of love while seeking only bonding could be compared to a couple who engages in intercourse only for the sake of procreation, while attempting to avoid all emotional attachment. Neither action would conform to God's designs for the gift of sexuality.

Few Christian couples go into marriage intending to have *no* children at all. Most understand that children are part of the point of marriage. Yet some feel that this means planning on trying to have children at some point rather than having each of their sexual acts ordered towards procreation. Although the purpose of the marital act is both union and procreation, some couples believe that it is possible to set aside one purpose and still fulfill the other. However, this is not sex as God intended it to be.

In Christian marriage, the purpose of the marital act extends beyond procreation to union—and, ultimately, to sanctification. *Sex is intended to make married couples holy.* That may sound strange, because our society falsely associates sex with what is dirty, risqué, and forbidden by God. But within marriage, the one-flesh union strengthens the bond between spouses, helping them to fulfill their God-given vocation. When a couple is pure of heart, this imbues the marital act with reverence. Only the chaste married couple is capable of experiencing the fullest power of this kind of union. When God's intention in creating sex is honored, marital intimacy helps them become saints.

If sex is designed for babies and bonding, why is it okay to have sex during non-fertile times of the month?

Because the Church is opposed to contraception, many people falsely assume that the Church thinks that sex is permissible only for the sake of having children. But God made women capable of conceiving only a few days of the month. Now, suppose God did not want married couples to have intercourse except when they are fertile. This means that the couple would have to abstain about twenty-five days per month, and if they did become pregnant, they would have to abstain for almost a year. Once the woman reached menopause and was no longer fertile, they could never again have marital relations.

God has not willed this because even when a woman is not fertile, the act of lovemaking still strengthens a marriage by uniting the spouses in a total gift of self. Regardless of fertility, the couple's gift to each other is a reflection of life-giving Trinitarian love, *provided* the couple does nothing to sterilize, interrupt, or obstruct their union. Therefore, it is morally licit for a married couple to make love even during times of infertility. Since they grow closer to God and to each other through the gift of sex, this will help them be better parents if God does bless them with children.

Still, it should be a personal decision. After all, it doesn't involve anyone else.

While the decision is indeed a personal one, the impact of your choice extends far beyond you. Like any sin, contracepting has implications for the family as well as society as a whole.

Consider what contraception has brought to society. As contraception became more accepted within the Christian community, the Catholic Church warned the world about the harm this would cause relationships. Marital infidelity would become more common, because spouses could be unfaithful without the fear of pregnancy. Since contraception offers an easy way to evade the consequences of breaking the moral law, there would also be a general lowering of morality, and the Church "feared that the man, growing used to the employment of anti-conceptive practices, may finally lose respect for the woman, and no longer caring for her physical and psychological equilibrium, may come to the point of considering her a mere instrument of selfish enjoyment, and no longer as his respected and beloved companion."[23]

With the increase in contraceptive use, it would become increasingly difficult to view sexuality as a sign of God's love. Furthermore, if people could divorce making love from making life, prohibitions against other kinds of sterile sexual activity (such as homosexual acts or masturbation) would no longer be reasonable.

Furthermore, contraception weakens a parent's ability to raise pure children. After all, how can parents credibly tell a child to follow the Church's teachings on sexuality *before* marriage if they are unwilling to obey the Church *within* marriage? Chastity is a virtue, and so it is more easily caught than it is taught. If parents want a child to practice self-control and purity, the most effective means to communicate these values is to model them. It has often been said that while children don't always obey their parents, they never fail to imitate them!

For all these reasons, contraception undermines civilization. Authentic marital love, on the other hand, holds a marriage together. A strong marriage holds the family together. Strong families hold society together, and a civilization will stand or fall upon this. "The future of humanity," according to the Church, "passes by way of the family."[24]

My priest says that the decision to use contraceptives is up to my conscience.

If this was his advice, then it was incomplete. Conscience inclines you to do good when you know what the good is. And yet, it is not enough to merely *desire* to do good. You must also *know* what is good and then *do* it. All three steps are necessary. For example, you would never hire a surgeon, a contractor, or even a taxi driver who lacked skills, but had good intentions and was willing to work. Just as knowledge is essential for the completion of a good work in natural affairs, it is equally necessary in supernatural matters as well.

The Church always insists that you listen to your conscience and obey it. However, we must first form our conscience in the truth—that is, according to the standards of God's law—and be willing to live according to the demands to which love calls us. Christ will speak clearly to us if we have the courage to listen to him. When a person does not form his conscience in the light of the truth, he is like a person driving at night without headlights and being sincere about not wanting to crash. Sincerity is good, but it's not enough.

Christopher West, respected Catholic authority on human sexuality, writes, "Love is not arbitrary. Love is not whatever we want it to be. Love is not merely an intense feeling or the sharing of pleasure. Love is to live according to the image in which we're made. Love is to give ourselves away freely, totally, faithfully, and fruitfully in imitation of Christ. Contraceptive intercourse contradicts all of this."[25]

Since the pope hasn't spoken infallibly about contraception, isn't it open for discussion?

Some doctrines of the Church are defined by an *ex cathedra* (infallible or "from the chair") statement by the pope. Others are taught infallibly by the magisterium.[26] The immorality of contraception is an example of a teaching that the Church has infallibly settled by means of the constant teaching of the ordinary magisterium. In the words of Saint John Paul II, "The Church's teaching on contraception does not belong in the category of matter open to free discussion among theologians. Teaching the contrary amounts to leading the moral consciences of spouses into error."[27]

Another Church document, the *Vademecum for Confessors,* also makes clear the definitive state of the Church's teaching: "The Church has always taught the intrinsic evil of contraception, that is, of every marital act intentionally rendered unfruitful. This teaching is to be held as definitive and irreformable."[28]

What authority does the Church have to tell us what to do in our marriage?

Veiled behind this question is a much deeper one: "What authority does the Church have in my life at all?" In all honesty, can we say that we have *ever* submitted our lives to the authority of the Church? Some Catholics will grant the Church authority over the rituals of their wedding ceremony, so long as the Church doesn't make demands once they get to the honeymoon suite. But as one man noted, "There are few better tests for whether or not someone lives a life in submission to God than what he or she does with their sexuality. Sex is such a powerful and meaningful desire that to give it up and obey God in that area is a true sign of worship."[29] To obey God when it comes to our sexuality is a true sign that we love and trust him more than we love and trust ourselves.

Since some of God's commandments involve sex, and Christ ordered his Church to teach all that he commands (Matt 28:20), the Church has the duty and authority to pass on to us what God has revealed about sexual morality. It is clear from Scripture that Jesus instituted a Church with such a mission. It would be unfaithful to Christ if it did not fulfill this calling.

In commissioning individuals to go and preach his message, Jesus emphasized: "He who hears you hears me, and he who rejects you rejects me" (Luke 10:16). Christ invested the Church with His own teaching authority because He knew that He would not be with the apostles on earth forever. He established a Church with bishops who "give instruction in sound doctrine" (Titus 1:9). The faithful are to submit to these spiritual leaders and defer to their authority (Heb. 13:17), so that they might not be led away by strange and diverse teachings. The authority of the apostles was passed on to bishops down through the ages as it had been to Joshua from Moses: through the imposition of hands (cf. Deut. 34:9).

The gates of hell would not prevail against this one Church (cf. Matt. 16:18), which is to be the pillar and foundation of truth (cf. 1 Tim. 3:15). The Holy Spirit guides the Church (cf. John 14:26) so that the she teaches what God entrusted to her. The Church guards his children as a mother watches over her young ones. The children may not always understand the mother's reasons for her rules, but they would do well to trust that her commands come from a loving heart and not a dictator's whims.

Does the Bible say anything about contraception?

Although the word "contraception" is never mentioned in Scripture, the act itself is condemned. For example, sterilization is condemned in Deuteronomy 23:1, and withdrawal is condemned in Genesis 38, in the story of Onan.

This story provides the clearest Scriptural case against contraception. In keeping with the custom of the time, Onan took his brother's widow as his own wife, to raise children in his dead brother's name. However, "whenever he had relations with [her], he wasted his seed on the ground" (Gen. 38:9, NAB) to ensure that pregnancy did not take place. The next verse tells us that God was "greatly offended" by Onan's actions, and struck him dead. Despite what the text plainly says, some argue that God killed him for failing to fulfill the levirate law (to give his brother's widow children). But Scripture indicates that the punishment for violating this law was public humiliation (cf. Deut. 25:5-10), not the death penalty. What if Onan had not wasted his seed but simply chose not to have intercourse? Would God have taken his life? Scripture says no.

Why would God take this event so seriously? Because desecrating the gift of our sexuality is a serious matter. Throughout the Bible, God uses the image of a bride and groom to give us a visible sign of his love for us. That is why the Church is called the "bride of Christ." Until the consummation of that union in heaven, the job of the married couple is to make the love of God visible on earth—through that total gift of self. In the words of the famous painter Salvador Dali, "The only way to make love is as a sacrament."[30]

The early Christians were well aware of the dignity of the marital act, and took seriously the command of scripture to "let the marriage bed be undefiled" (Heb 13:4). Because of this, they were explicit in their condemnation of contraception. Around A.D. 195, Clement of Alexandria wrote, "Because of its divine institution for the propagation of man, the seed is not to be vainly ejaculated, nor is it to be damaged, nor is it to be wasted."[31] Hippolytus of Rome in 255 referred to those who used drugs of sterility as the "so-called faithful."[32]

In the fifth century, St. Augustine wrote, "I am supposing, then, although you are not lying [with your wife] for the sake of procreating offspring, you are not for the sake of lust obstructing their procreation by an evil prayer or an evil deed. Those who do this, although they are called husband and wife, are not; nor do they retain any reality of marriage, but with a respectable name cover a shame. Sometimes this lustful cruelty, or cruel lust, comes to this, that they even procure poisons of sterility [i.e., contraceptives] . . . Assuredly if both husband and wife are like this, they are not married, and if they were like this from the beginning, they come together not joined in matrimony, but in seduction."[33]

This Christian teaching continued through the ages, and even the Protestant Reformers and other religious leaders condemned contraception. Martin Luther said, "The exceedingly foul deed of Onan, the basest of wretches . . . is a most disgraceful sin. It is far more atrocious than incest and adultery. We call it unchastity, yes, a sodomistic sin. For Onan goes in to her; that is, he lies with her and copulates, and when it comes to the point of insemination, spills the semen, lest the woman conceive. Surely at such a time the order of nature established by God in procreation should be followed. Accordingly, it was a most disgraceful crime . . . Consequently, he deserved to be killed by God. He committed an evil deed. Therefore, God punished him."[34] John Calvin seconded Luther, calling contraception "monstrous,"[35] and John Wesley said that those who commit the sin of Onan dishonor their body and "destroy their own souls."[36]

Such disdain towards contraception extended beyond Christianity. Gandhi said, "Man has sufficiently degraded women for his lust, and contraception, no matter how well meaning the advocates may be, will still further degrade her."[37] He added, "Self-indulgence with contraceptives may prevent the coming of children but will sap the vitality of both men and women, perhaps more of men than of women."[38]

How is using NFP to space births different from contracepting?

Let's suppose that a married couple is using contraceptives for the same reason another couple is practicing NFP. Both couples already have children, and hope to have more. But for good reasons, they need to space out the next birth by a couple of years. Both couples have the same intent. However, the good intent of a couple is not sufficient to determine the morality of their act.

By way of comparison, if two women wanted to avoid becoming overweight, one might go on a diet and the other might engage in binging and purging (bulimia). Both may stay slim, but one exercised the virtue of temperance while the other committed the unhealthy practice of gluttony coupled with the physically damaging practice of induced vomiting.[39]

Similarly, the Church rejects contraception not because a couple necessarily has bad intentions—but because the *means* they use to accomplish their goal is immoral. Married couples are free to have intercourse (or to agree to abstain from it) on any given day, regardless of the wife's fertility. But when they do join as one flesh, they must not frustrate God's designs. It is God alone who has the power to create an immortal soul as a result of the marital act, and to contracept is to say that God's presence is not desired. Instead of honoring God as the "Lord and giver of life," contraception eliminates his role in the marital act. Clearly, then, a couple abstaining from sex for a just reason cannot be compared to a couple who sterilizes their acts of lovemaking in order to take the pleasure of the sexual act in isolation.

The Church is not opposed to contraception because it is artificial. After all, the Church allows the use of countless artificial drugs and other technological advances. However, these are to be used to heal dysfunction and promote the proper functioning of the body as God ordained it. Contraception does the opposite: It prevents the proper and healthy functioning of one bodily system (the reproductive system), inducing or simulating a dysfunctional state (sterility).

Therefore, there is a vast moral difference between NFP and contraception. Contraception deliberately interrupts, sterilizes, and works against (*contra*) the marital act as God designed it, while NFP does not. Couples who practice NFP respect God's plan for sex, including a woman's fertility, and work *with* that plan to space births.

One husband remarked that there are legitimate reasons to delay pregnancy, "but God has taken care of that already. So deeply has he wrought his purposes into us that a woman's body not only bears fruit but has seasons . . . providing not only for bringing babies forth but for spacing them. There is no need to thwart the design, to artificially block fertility during a naturally fertile time. One only has to wait for a few days. If that is too difficult for us, something is wrong."[40]

If you feel that there is no moral difference between the two methods, why not practice NFP? Immediately, you may point out that contraception is easier to use and more convenient. Indeed, NFP is more demanding. It requires discipline, patience, sacrifice and commitment to the will of God. But because NFP's *manner* of spacing births is so different than that of contraception, it should lead one to see that there is also great *moral* difference between the two.[41]

Still another moral difference between contraception and NFP is the fact that some birth control methods can cause early abortions. For example: the IUD,[42] the Patch,[43] Implanon,[44] NuvaRing,[45] Depo-Provera,[46] the "morning after pill,"[47] and the birth control pill[48] sometimes operate by preventing a newly conceived child from attaching to the uterus. This results in a first-trimester abortion—without the mother even knowing it.

Unfortunately, not all doctors are aware that these drugs can be abortifacients. Walter Larimore, M.D. admitted that he prescribed the pill for nearly twenty years—and used it in his own marriage—before anyone informed him that it could have such an effect. When another doctor clued him in, he said that he had never heard of such a thing, and that the claims seemed to be "outlandish, excessive, and inaccurate."[49]

So, he began a search of the medical literature, "to disprove these claims to my partner, myself, and any patients who might ask about it." However, what he discovered compelled him to stop using the pill in his medical and personal life. In his quest for information, he realized how many doctors (and patients) were ignorant of the abortifacient potential of the pill. It was a humbling realization, considering that ever since the 1970's, the patient package insert for birth control pills explained how the drug reduces the likelihood of implantation.[50] After informing his colleagues, Dr. Larimore noted, "several said that they thought it would change the way family physicians informed their patients about the Pill and its potential effects."[51]

Lastly, contraceptives also have a number of adverse side effects that NFP does not. Each method of contraception carries with it some risk of harmful side effects, many of which are downplayed in our contraceptive culture. One example is the link between the Pill and breast cancer. Some risks are more common than others, but men and women need to be accurately forewarned of all of the possible consequences.

Our doctor told us that birth control is safe. Why should we think otherwise?

Consider the following possible side-effects of contraception, and then ask yourself if you would consider these methods "safe":

Birth Control Pills
- According to the journal of the Mayo Clinic, 21 of 23 studies of women who took the Pill prior to

having their first baby showed that such women increased their risk of developing breast cancer.[52] The link to breast cancer has also been acknowledged by the companies that make birth control pills and the World Health Organization.[53]

- The Pill also increases a woman's risk of cervical cancer,[54] liver cancer,[55] and potentially fatal blood clots.[56]
- A common complaint of Pill users is a decrease in one's sex drive. Part of this is because the Pill increases a woman's level of SHBG (sex hormone binding globulin),[57] which decreases the amount of testosterone available in her body. It had been thought that this undesirable side-effect would be reversible. However, research published in *The Journal of Sexual Medicine* showed that the levels of SHBG were still twice as high in women a year after going off the Pill.[58] In an article entitled "Can taking the pill dull a woman's desire forever?" the same scientists feared, "There's the possibility it is imprinting a woman for the rest of her life."[59]

Condom

- According to *The Journal of the American Medical Association*, women who use barrier methods of birth control are more than twice as likely to suffer preeclampsia during childbirth.[60] Here's why: During intercourse, the woman's immune system develops a tolerance to the man's sperm and seminal fluid.[61] For several hours after intercourse, a woman's immune cells will collect and transfer a man's foreign proteins and entire sperm cells from her cervix to her lymph nodes, where her immune system learns to recognize his genes.[62] However, if the couple decides to use a barrier method of birth control for an extended period of time before having children, the womb will not be accustomed to the sperm, and the woman's immune system may treat them as foreign bodies. This can disrupt the delicate balance of hormones, and cause the woman's blood vessels to constrict, leading to higher blood pressure in the expectant mother.[63] This condition (preeclampsia) is the third leading cause of women dying during childbirth.[64] However, a man's semen offers a protective effect against preeclampsia, because the woman's immune system is more likely to recognize his baby. So in a certain sense, couples who use the condom are having *unprotected* sexual intercourse, because the man is not protecting the woman's body with the beneficial effects of his semen.[65]

Depo-Provera (The Shot)

- Women have sued the makers of the shot for 700 million dollars.[66] One reason for this is because the shot thins out a woman's bones.[67] After years of receiving birth control injections, a young woman could have the bones of a 50 to 60 year old. For this reason, the FDA has attached a "Black Box Warning" to the shot, which is the most serious warning that can be attached to a prescription drug.[68]

- According to the company that makes the birth control shot, children born to women on Depo-Provera are more likely to have webbed toes and fingers, and chromosomal anomalies. The boys are twice as likely to have genital deformities, and the baby girls are more likely to suffer masculinizing effects of the drug's chemicals, causing genital abnormalities.[69]
- Because of its link to breast cancer, veterinarians stopped prescribing Depo-Provera for dogs.[70] However, it's still being given to women, and is often injected into child molesters as a punishment to decrease their sex drive![71]

Ortho Evra (The Patch)
- The Associated Press reported in 2005 that they petitioned the FDA for a database containing 16,000 different reports of adverse reactions to the patch. Within the reports were 23 deaths associated with the patch, 17 of them blood clot-related.[72]
- Because of the numerous side effects of the birth control patch,[73] the makers of the product are facing lawsuits related to deaths and other injuries from thousands of women.[74]

Sterilization
- Men who have vasectomies may be two-and-a-half times as likely to develop kidney stones.[75]
- Following a vasectomy, a man's testes will continue to produce millions of sperm each day. However, because the vasa deferentia have been severed or blocked, the sperm have no natural way to be released. If the tubes are blocked, the pressure of sperm being backed up often causes a blowout of the epididymis, which can be very painful. Inevitably, sperm cells enter the bloodstream, where antibodies are created to destroy them.
- Sterilization surgeries are much more risky for women than for men, because the procedure is more invasive. Not surprisingly, the more education a woman receives, the less likely she is to sterilize herself.[76]
- Men and women who undergo sterilization often suffer from the guilt and regret of mutilating their bodies. They often experience reduced marital satisfaction.

For more information about these—and other—forms of contraception, visit chastity.com.

If we choose to use NFP, How do we know if our reasons to avoid pregnancy are valid from the Church's perspective?

Because NFP is so effective in regulating births, it is

possible for couples using NFP to have "a contraceptive mentality" and close themselves off from the gift of life. Therefore, NFP must be practiced responsibly, used to space births only when there is a just reason to do so.

The size of each family is something that can only be determined by the couple. Therefore, neither the Church nor the state can impose a limit or expectation on the number of children. However, the Church encourages couples to have a just reason to space births and to be sure their decision is "not motivated by selfishness but is in conformity with the generosity appropriate to responsible parenthood."[77] In planning a family, a couple should consider the interests of their family, society as a whole, and the Church. Bear in mind that these interests include not only material needs but spiritual ones as well. Saint John Paul II says:

"Decisions about the number of children and the sacrifices to be made for them must not be taken only with a view to adding comfort and preserving a peaceful existence. Reflecting upon this mater before God, with the graces drawn from the Sacrament, and guided by the teaching of the Church, parents will remind themselves that it is certainly less serious to deny their children certain comforts or material advantages than to deprive them of the presence of brothers or sisters who could help them to grow in humanity and to realize the beauty of life at all ages and in all its variety."[78]

As the Holy Father implied, the gift of siblings is irreplaceable. While at a local playground, a mother of a four-year-old only child saw that I had two sons under the age of four, and asked, "How do you do it? We only have one little girl and I'm exhausted." As my boys chased each other in countless laps around the slide, I thought to myself, "Perhaps you're so tired because you have to be mom while playing the role of a two-year-old sister all day long."

Unfortunately, modern culture is imbued with a contraceptive mentality that sees children as deductions instead of additions. Not long ago, when I announced to someone that my wife and I were expecting a baby girl, she remarked, "That's good. You had the boys, and now you've got your girl." I was tempted to remark, "Yea. Now I've got the whole set, so I can stop collecting." It made me wonder how many people are having children simply for their own sakes.

On another occasion, I told an acquaintance that my wife and I were expecting our third child. With bulging eyes, he remarked, "Three? So, you guys are done, right?" If I had told him that we were buying a third car or a three-story house, he wouldn't have flinched. But three kids? That's downright self-indulgent and irresponsible! Or is it? Provided my wife and I are able to care for them—and retain some semblance of sanity for ourselves—there is no greater gift that we could give them than the gift of life. In exchange, they save us from ourselves, give us unimaginable joy, and teach us to love.

As a married couple ages, you never seem to hear them complain that they had too many kids. Could you imagine a mother or father saying, "Yeah, we probably should have stopped at two. Numbers three through five really decreased our quality of life"? If anything, couples often regret having had too few.

I once read of a mother in her forties who raised a small family. She would sit at the dinner table with her children and think to herself that someone was missing. Had she known when she was young how priceless each life would be, she may have been willing to sacrifice a few more years of sleepless nights in order to have just one more child.

Why is it wrong to want to have control over my own body?

The Church recognizes our right to have control over our bodies. Only by having control over one's body is a person is able to make a gift of oneself.

Unfortunately, the contraception industry would like its customers to believe that contraception grants them control over their bodies and relationships and freedom in their sex lives. But contraception cannot be considered any more "freeing" than castration. Freedom can be attained only through self-control.

Contraception can never make women free. To treat pregnancy as if it were a disease implies that there is something defective in the way women are created—that a woman's fertility is a burden. That is not a very liberating experience for any woman. NFP is a beautiful alternative because it doesn't treat a woman's body as if it needs to be subdued by drugs or shielded behind latex barriers. It invites the man to treat the woman's fertility with reverence instead of disdain. This is true sexual liberation.

In the words of Christopher West, "If the real problem behind women's oppression is men's failure to treat them properly as persons, contraception is a sure way to keep women in chains."[79] The earliest feminists opposed contraception for this very reason, and some modern feminists still realize that contraception is the enemy of women's liberation.[80]

To be fair, not every woman who uses contraception feels used by her husband, and couples using NFP can struggle with selfishness as well. Even so, only the couple living the virtue of chastity—using sex according to God's plan—is able to be truly free. Only virtue frees you from important questions such as these: "Am I harming my (spouse's) body?" "Are we offending God?"

Freed from these restraints and living with a calm conscience, a couple is free to glorify God in their bodies and experience the joy of making God's love present each time they express their union as one flesh.

If you desire freedom, only a life of virtue can fulfill you. God has given us the gift of freedom in order to use it for the sake of love, not in order to escape the demands of love. In the words of Saint John Paul II, "Once the truth is denied to human beings, it is pure illusion to try to set them free. Truth and freedom either go together hand in hand or together they perish in misery."[81]

To think that one becomes free when he acts against God's laws is like thinking that a driver becomes most free when he disregards the guardrail and sails off a cliff. Illusory freedom such as this robs us of having God's best in our lives. Only when we submit our wills to the truth about love will we be set free.

What does the Church teach about practices to aid in fertility, such as fertility drugs *in-vitro* fertilization, or artificial insemination?

Medical technology exists to promote the proper functioning of our bodies. Since infertility is a dysfunction of a woman's reproductive system, using drugs and even surgery to promote healthy functioning of the reproductive system can be morally acceptable. However, these measures must be used responsibly. For example, while using fertility drugs may be permissible, a couple must consider all possible outcomes. If more than one egg is fertilized, carrying them all to term is permissible—destroying fertilized eggs via "selective reduction" (another word for "abortion") is not.

Although some people expect fertility to flip on and off like a light switch, no one but God has absolute control over the gift of life. When couples lose sight of this, they sometimes take matters into their own hands, and begin to see children as a *right*. What follows is often an unbridled attempt to bring life into the world, even at the expense of their unborn children. In order to obtain one child, many others are often discarded.

In an address to President George W. Bush, Saint John Paul II said that man must be "the master, not the product, of his technology."[82] While the Church acknowledges that some measures are permissible to bring healing to the reproductive system, medical procedures such as *in vitro* fertilization and artificial insemination are not. There are several important reasons for this:

- *It violates the child's dignity and the marital union.* Artificial insemination involves taking the sperm from a man and injecting it into the uterus or placing it in the woman's cervix. However, each child should be brought into being by an act of love between his parents, not from a researcher tinkering with cells in a Petri dish. When the sperm are taken from a man other than the husband, it infringes upon the child's right to be born of a father and mother known to him, and it betrays the spouses' marital pledge to become a father and mother only through each other. (In addition, many states do not require STD testing for sperm donors, so HIV and other viruses can be spread during the process.)

- *It kills many unborn children.* IVF involves conceiving life in a laboratory and transferring the fertilized eggs into a woman's womb. This process kills many unborn children. Extra embryos are fertilized during the procedure, which are often frozen and kept for a later attempt, donated, experimented on, or destroyed. Other times, embryos that are placed in the womb using IVF frequently fail to implant there. It's obviously immoral to create and destroy so many lives in an attempt to bring one to life.

- *It separates the unitive and procreative aspects of sexuality.* Reproductive technology may assist the sexual act in conceiving new life, but must never *replace* it. In other words, just as contraception tries to make love without making babies, so IVF and artificial insemination attempt to make babies without making love. Neither act is moral, because life and love are inseparable.

If these methods are immoral, then why does God let conception occur?

God has entrusted us with the gift of sexuality, and he won't prevent us from abusing that freedom. For example, if a child is conceived out of wedlock, the act is immoral, but God still allows life to come forth from it. Just because conception occurs, we can't conclude from this that the means to bring about this end was good. In fact, of all of the ways to bring life into the world (marital love, fornication, adultery, rape, incest, IVF, artificial insemination, etc.) only one (married love) fully respects the dignity of the human person and God's gift of sexuality.

Many are led to believe that IVF and artificial insemination are the only options available to an infertile couple hoping to have a child of their own. This is not the case, because there are many doctors who specialize in finding the cause of infertility and healing the woman or man instead of replacing their infertility with technology. For example, see The Saint Paul VI Institute (popepaulvi.com.)

Couples unable to conceive need not give up hope of becoming parents. Adoptions, both domestic and international, are commonplace. Foster parenting is another, less costly option that brings life and hope to children in desperate need of loving homes. The *Catechism of the Catholic Church* encourages infertile couples to "unite themselves with the Lord's Cross, the source of all spiritual fecundity. They can give expression to their generosity by adopting abandoned children"[83]

Is it acceptable to use contraceptives for strictly medicinal purposes?

Hormonal birth control does have other, legitimate medical applications that have nothing to do with contraception. For example, the Pill is often prescribed to treat conditions such as endometriosis, ovarian cysts, irregular cycles, and painful cramps. In some cases, women suffering from these conditions may lawfully use the Pill in spite of its contraceptive effects, as long as the contraceptive effects are not intended. However, these conditions often have alternative remedies without the contraceptive effects or adverse side effects of hormonal birth control. If an alternative remedy exists, it should be preferred. The Saint Paul VI Institute specializes in such alternatives, so you may wish to contact them through the information on the previous page. The NFP-Only Directory at onemoresoul.com is a helpful resource as well.

Where do we go from here?

First, if you are currently using contraception, stop. Take this to prayer, go to confession, and present this booklet to your spouse. Should he or she be willing to learn about NFP, take an NFP class together. Your parish or diocese should offer these for any interested couples, and you can ask your priest how to sign up for one.

If your spouse refuses to stop using contraception, then you are not morally responsible for his or her choice. As long as you are not doing something immoral, you may, for the sake of the marriage, still engage in the marital act. However, the Church states, "It is necessary to carefully evaluate the question of cooperation in evil when recourse is made to means which can have an abortifacient effect."[84] Continue to pray for and dialogue with your spouse, so that his or her heart will change on the matter.

Although many spouses report that NFP deepened their intimacy, it is not uncommon for it to also create challenges within marriage. Do not despair if you experience this. One of the purposes of marriage is the sanctification of the spouses, and NFP will often play a role this process, bringing to the surface areas within the relationship and within each person that may need healing and purification.

NFP is a demanding sacrifice at times, but by being so generous with God, there is no doubt that He will bless you: "Give, and it will be given to you; good measure, pressed down, shaken together, running over, will be put into your lap. For the measure you give will be the measure you get back" (Luke 6:38). It is a sacrifice, but in the words of Saint John Paul II, "it is through the cross that the family can attain the fullness of its being and the perfection of its love."[85]

May God bless you with a happy marriage and a holy family.

1. Cf. P. Frank-Herrmann, et al., "The Effectiveness of a Fertility Awareness Based Method to Avoid Pregnancy in Relation to a Couple's Sexual Behaviour During the Fertile Time: A Prospective Longitudinal Study," *Human Reproduction* doi:10.1093/humrep/dem003 (February 2007): 1–10; R. E. J. Ryder, "'Natural Family Planning': Effective Birth Control Supported by the Catholic Church," *British Medical Journal* 307 (1993): 723–726.
2. Ryder, "Natural Family Planning," 725.
3. Cf. Mercedes Arzú Wilson, "The Practice of Natural Family Planning Versus the Use of Artificial Birth Control: Family, Sexual, and Moral Issues," *Catholic Social Science Review* 7 (November 2002); Couple to Couple League, "What's Wrong with Contraception?"
4. Nona Aguilar, *No-Pill No-Risk Birth Control* (New York: Rawson & Wade, 1980), 102.
5. Cyril Jones-Kellett, "Charger Quarterback Lends Voice to Chastity Conference," *The Southern Cross* (June 21, 2007), 11.
6. Charlotte Hays, "Solving the Puzzle of Natural Family Planning," *Crisis*, December 2001, 15.
7. *Faithful to Each Other For Ever: A Catholic Handbook of Pastoral Help for Marriage Preparation* (Washington D.C.: United States Catholic Conference, 1989), 46.
8. *Humanae Vitae* 21.
9. Cf. Irit Sinai and Marcos Arévalo, "It's All in the Timing: Coital Frequency and Fertility Awareness-Based Methods of Family Planning," *Journal of Biosocial Science* 38:6 (November 2006): 763–777.
10. Cf. R.A. Hatcher, et al., *Contraceptive Technology: Nineteenth Revised Edition* (New York, N.Y.: Ardent Media, 2007).
11. Cf. Thomas Hilgers, et al., "Creighton Model NaProEducation Technology for Avoiding Pregnancy. Use Effectiveness," *The Journal of Reproductive Medicine* 43:6 (June 1998): 495–502.
12. John Paul II, "True Human Love Reflects the Divine," September 25, 1993.
13. Cf. Baylor College of Medicine, "Evolution and Revolution: The Past, Present, and Future of Contraception," *The Contraception Report* 10:6 (February 2000): 16.

14 Cf. Andrea Tone, "Contraceptive Consumers: Gender and the Political Economy of Birth Control in the 1930s," *Journal of Social History* (Spring 1996).

15 Cf. "Contraception and Sterilization" (www.catholic.com/library/contraception_and_sterilization.asp).

16 Patrick Fagan, "A 'Culture' of Inverted Sexuality," *Catholic World Report* (November 1998).

17 Patrick Fagan, "A 'Culture' of Inverted Sexuality," *Catholic World Report* (November 1998).

18 Patrick Fagan, "A 'Culture' of Inverted Sexuality," *Catholic World Report* (November 1998).

19 Frank Sheed, *Society and Sanity* (New York: Sheed and Ward, 1953), 107.

20 Karol Wojtyla, *The Way to Christ* (San Francisco: Harper, 1982), 55–56.

21 Cf. Janet E. Smith, *Contraception: Why Not?* (Dayton, Ohio: One More Soul, 1999).

22 Cf. *Catechism of the Catholic Church* 2363.

23 HV 17.

24 *Familiaris Consortio* 86.

25 Christopher West, *Good News about Sex and Marriage* (Ann Arbor, Mich.: Servant Publications, 2000), 110.

26 Cf. *Lumen Gentium* 25.

27 John Paul II, "The Church's Teaching on Contraception is not a Matter for Free Discussion among Theologians," *L'Osservatore Romano* (6 July 1987).

28 *Vademecum for Confessors concerning Some Aspects of the Morality of Conjugal Life*, 2:4, par. 33.

29 Henry Cloud and John Townsend, *Boundaries in Dating* (Grand Rapids, Mich.: Zondervan, 2000), 252.

30 *Time* (European edition), November 10, 1980, 64, as quoted in Donald DeMarco, *New Perspectives on Contraception* (Dayton, OH.: One More Soul, 1999), 54.

31 Clement of Alexandria, *The Instructor of Children* 2:10:91:2.

32 Hippolytus of Rome, *Refutation of All Heresies* 9:12.

33 Augustine, *Marriage and Concupiscence* 1:15:17.

34 Martin Luther, in *Luther's Works*, vol. 7, pp. 20-21, as quoted in Charles D. Provan, *The Bible and Birth Control* (Monogahela, Pa: Zimmer Printing, 1989), 14.

35 John Calvin, *Commentary on Genesis 38:8-10* (Latin translation), as quoted in Provan, *The Bible and Birth Control*, 15.

36 John Wesley, *Commentary on Genesis, 38:7*, as quoted in Provan, *The Bible and Birth Control,* 91.

37 West, *Good News*, 119.

38 Mahatma Gandhi, *Wisdom for all Time: Mahatma Gandhi and Pope Paul VI on Birth Regulation*, prepared by A.S. Antonisamy, (Pondicherry, India: Family Life Service Center, 1978), 26, as quoted in DeMarco, *New Perspectives*, 86.

39 Cf. Couple to Couple League, "What's Wrong with Contraception?"; Smith, *Contraception*.

40 J. Budziszewski, in Sam and Bethany Torode, *Open Embrace* (Grand Rapids, Mich.: Eerdmans, 2002), xvi.

41 Cf. Janet E. Smith, *Contraception: Why Not?* (Dayton, Ohio: One More Soul, 1999).

42 Cf. ParaGard Patient Package Information, Duramed Pharmaceuticals, Inc, (May 2006); J.B. Stanford and R.T. Mikolajczyk, "Mechanisms of Action of Intrauterine Devices: Update and Estimation of Postfertilization Effects," *American Journal of Obstetrics and Gynecology* 187:6 (December 2002): 1699-1708; Y.C. *Smart,* et al., "Early Pregnancy Factor as a Monitor for Fertilization in Women Wearing Intrauterine Devices," *Fertility and Sterility* 37:2 (February 1982): 201-204.

43 Cf. *Physicians' Desk Reference*, (Montvale, N.J.: Thomson, 2006), 2402.

44 Cf. Implanon Patient Insert, Organon USA, Inc., (July 2006), 1.

45 Cf. NuvaRing Physician's Insert, Organon USA Inc. (2005).

46 Cf. *Physicians' Desk Reference*, (Montvale, N.J.: Thomson, 2006): 2620.

47 Cf. *Physicians' Desk Reference*, (Montvale, N.J.: Thomson, 2006): 1068; Chris Kahlenborn, et al., "Postfertilization Effect of Hormonal Emergency Contraception," *The Annals of Pharmacotherapy* 36 (March 2002): 465-470; Department of Health and Human Services, *Federal Register* Notice 62:37 (25 February 1997): 8611.

48. Cf. Larimore, et al., "Postfertilization Effects of Oral Contraceptives and Their Relationship to Informed Consent," *Archives of Family Medicine* 9 (2000): 126–133; *Physicians' Desk Reference*, (Montvale, N.J.: Thomson, 2006): 2414.
49. Walter Larimore and Joseph Stanford, "Postfertilization Effects of Oral Contraceptives and Their Relationship to Informed Consent," *Archives of Family Medicine* 9 (February 2000): 133.
50. Cf. *Federal Register* 41:236 (7 December 1976): 53,634.
51. Walter Larimore and Joseph Stanford, "Postfertilization Effects of Oral Contraceptives and Their Relationship to Informed Consent," *Archives of Family Medicine* 9 (February 2000): 133.
52. Cf. Chris Kahlenborn, et al., "Oral Contraceptive Use as a Risk Factor for Premenopausal Breast Cancer: A Meta-analysis," *Mayo Clinic Proceedings* 81:10 (October 2006): 1290–1302.
53. Cf. *Physicians' Desk Reference*, (Montvale, N.J.: Thomson, 2006) 2415; World Health Organization, "IARC Monographs Programme Finds Combined Estrogen-Progestogen Contraceptives and Menopausal Therapy are Carcinogenic to Humans," International Agency for Research on Cancer, Press Release 167 (29 July 2005).
54. Cf. Smith, et al., "Cervical Cancer and Use of Hormonal Contraceptives: A Systematic Review," *Lancet* 361 (2003): 1159–1167.
55. Cf. World Health Organization, "IARC Monographs Programme Finds Combined Estrogen-Progestogen Contraceptives and Menopausal Therapy are Carcinogenic to Humans," International Agency for Research on Cancer, Press Release 167 (29 July 2005); La Vecchia, "Oral contraceptives and cancer," *Minerva Ginecologica* 58:3 (June 2006): 209–214.
56. Cf. *Physicians' Desk Reference*, 2415; Kemmeren, et al., "Third Generation Oral Contraceptives and Risk of Venous Thrombosis: Meta Analysis," *British Medical Journal* 323 (July 2001): 131–134; Parkin, et al., "Oral Contraceptives and Fatal Pulmonary Embolism," *The Lancet* 355:9221 (June 2000): 2133–2134; Hedenmalm, et al., "Fatal Venous Thromboembolism Associated with Different Combined Oral Contraceptives," *Drug Safety* 28:10 (2005): 907–916; Sameuelsson, et al., "Mortality from Venous

Thromboembolism in Young Swedish Women and its Relation to Pregnancy and Use of Oral Contraceptives," *European Journal of Epidemiology* 20:6 (2005): 509–516.

57 Cf. *Physicians' Desk Reference*, (Montvale, N.J.: Thomson, 2006), 2414; Julia Warnock, et al., "Comparison of Androgens in Women with Hypoactive Sexual Desire Disorder: Those on Combined Oral Contraceptives (COCs) vs. Those not on COCs," *The Journal of Sexual Medicine* 3:5 (September 2006): 878–882.

58 Cf. Panzer, et al., "Impact of Oral Contraceptives on Sex Hormone-Binding Globulin and Androgen Levels: A Retrospective Study in Women with Sexual Dysfunction," *Journal of Sexual Medicine* 3:1 (January 2006): 104–113.

59 "Can Taking the Pill Dull a Woman's Desire Forever?" *New Scientist* (27 May 2005), 17.

60 Cf. H.S. Klonoff-Cohen, et al., "An Epidemiologic Study of Contraception and Preeclampsia," *The Journal of the American Medical Association* 262:22 (8 December 1989): 3143–3147.

61 Cf. S.A. Robertson, et al., "Transforming Growth Factor Beta—A Mediator of Immune Deviation in Seminal Plasma," *Journal of Reproductive Immunology* 57:1–2 (October/November 2002): 109–128.

62 Cf. Douglas Fox, "Gentle Persuasion," *New Scientist* (9 February 2002); Douglas Fox, "Why Sex, Really?" *U.S. News and World Report* (21 October 2002): 60–62.

63 Cf. S.A. Robertson, et al., "The Role of Semen in Induction of Maternal Immune Tolerance to Pregnancy," *Seminars in Immunology* 13 (2001): 243; John B Wilks, *A Consumer's Guide to the Pill and Other Drugs* 2nd ed. (Stafford, Virginia: American Life League, Inc., 1997), 136.

64 Cf. A. Hirozawa, "Preeclampisa and Eclampsia, While Often Preventable, Are Among Top Causes of Pregnancy-Related Deaths," *Family Planning Perspectives* 33:4 (July/August 2001): 182; Andrea Mackay, et al., "Pregnancy-Related Mortality From Preeclampsia and Eclampsia," *Obstetrics & Gynecology* 97 (2001): 533–538.

65 Cf. S.A. Robertson, et al., "Seminal 'Priming' for Protection from Pre-Eclampsia-A Unifying Hypothesis," *Journal of Reproductive*

Immunology 59:2 (August 2003): 253–265; G.R. Verwoerd, et al., "Primipaternity and Duration of Exposure to Sperm Antigens as Risk Factors for Pre-eclamsia," *International Journal of Gynaecology and Obstetrics* 78:2 (August 2002): 121–126; J. I. Einarsson, et al., "Sperm Exposure and Development of Preeclampsia," *American Journal of Obstetrics and Gynecology* 188:5 (May 2003): 1241–1243; M. Hernandez-Valencia, et al., "[Barrier Family Planning Methods as Risk Factors Which Predisposes to Preeclampsia]," *Ginecologia y Obstetrica de Mexico* 68 (August 2000): 333–338; Dekker, et al., "Immune Maladaptation in the Etiology of Preeclampsia: A Review of Corroborative Epidemiologic Studies," *Obstetrical and Gynecological Survey* 53:6 (June 1998): 377–382.

66 CTV.ca News, "Class Action Suit Filed Over Birth Control Drug," (19 December 2005).

67 Cf. U.S. Food and Drug Administration, "Black Box Warning Added Concerning Long-Term Use of Depo-Provera Contraceptive Injection," FDA Talk Paper (17 November 2004).

68 Cf. U.S. Food and Drug Administration, "Black Box Warning Added Concerning Long-Term Use of Depo-Provera Contraceptive Injection," FDA Talk Paper (17 November 2004).

69 Cf. Physician Information, Depo-Provera CI, Pharmacia & Upjohn Company (November 2004); Patient Labeling, Pharmacia & Upjohn Company, October 2004.

70 Cf. "The Case Against Depo-Provera: Problems in the U.S.," *Multinational Monitor* 6:2–3 (February/March 1985); Depo-Provera, Patient Labeling, Pharmacia & Upjohn Company (October 2004).

71 Cf. T.A. Kiersch, "Treatment of Sex Offenders with Depo-Provera," *The Bulletin of the American Academy of Psychiatry and the Law* 18:2 (1990): 179–187; Assembly Bill 3339, "An act to repeal and add Section 645 of the Penal Code, relating to crimes," California State Senate, Amended 20 August 1996; 2005; California Penal Code, 645.

72 Cf. Associated Press, "Birth Control Patch Linked to Higher Fatality Rate," MSNBC (17 July 2005).

73 Cf. U.S Food and Drug Administration, "Ortho Evra (norelgestromin/ethinyl estradiol) Information," Department of Health and Human Services (20 September 2006).

74 Cf. Johnson & Johnson, SEC Filing, Annual Report for Period Ending 12/31/07; Associated Press, "Birth control patch linked to higher fatality rate," 20 July 2005.

75 Cf. R.A. Kronmal, et al., "Vasectomy and Urolithiasis," *The Lancet* 331 (1988): 22–23.

76 Cf. William Mosher, et al., "Use of Contraception and Use of Family Planning Services in the United States: 1982-2002," *Advance Data From Vital and Health Statistics* 350, Centers for Disease Control (10 December 2004): 10.

77 CCC 2368.

78 John Paul II, homily on the Washington Mall, October 7, 1979, as quoted in John F. Kippley, *Marriage Is for Keeps* (Cincinnati, Ohio: Foundation for the Family, 1994), 73.

79 West, *Good News*, 122.

80 Cf. Donald DeMarco "Contraception and the Trivalization of Sex." (www.cuf.org)

81 *Fides et Ratio*, 90.

82 Address to President Bush at Castel Gondolfo, (23 July 2008)

83 CCC, 2379.

84 For more information, see *Vademecum for Confessors*, Pontifical Council for the Family, 13:3 (12 February 1997).

85 *Familiaris Consortio*, 86.

GOT QUESTIONS? GET ANSWERS.

WATCH VIDEOS
GET RELATIONSHIP ADVICE
LAUNCH A PROJECT
READ ANSWERS TO TOUGH QUESTIONS
FIND HELP TO HEAL FROM THE PAST
LISTEN TO POWERFUL TESTIMONIES
SHOP FOR GREAT RESOURCES
SCHEDULE A SPEAKER

THE SEXUAL CULTURE WAR IS ON

SEXTING, FACEBOOK GOSSIP, PORNOGRAPHY, HOOKING UP, BROKEN FAMILIES, AND BROKEN HEARTS.

HOW DO YOU TURN PEER PRESSURE INTO PURE PRESSURE?

Jason and Crystalina Evert have spoken to more than one million teens on five continents. Now, schedule a presentation to have them inspire the youth in your junior high, high school, university, church, or conference.

Teens today need straight answers to tough questions about dating, relationships, and sexual purity. That's why Chastity Project offers more than a dozen presentations designed to empower students and parents.

FOR MORE INFORMATION, VISIT

FOR $3 OR LESS, WHO WOULD YOU GIVE THESE BOOKS AND CDS TO?

In order to reach as many people as possible, more than 40 chastity CDs and books are available in bulk orders for $3 or less! Therefore, share this book and others like it with the people in your life who need it right now. For example:

YOUR COLLEGE DORM | YOUR HIGH SCHOOL
YOUR YOUTH OR YOUNG ADULT GROUP AT CHURCH | YOUR ALMA MATER

Buy a case of books and donate them as gifts at graduation, freshman orientation, retreats, conferences, confirmation, as a missionary effort through campus ministry, or to people you meet anywhere. You never know whose life you could change.

TO ORDER, VISIT

Printed by Libri Plureos GmbH in Hamburg, Germany